Little Pebble™

Our Amazing Senses

Our Mouths Can Taste

T0052419

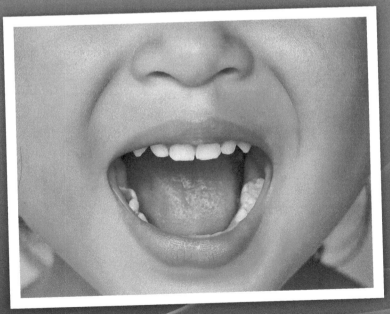

by Jodi Wheeler-Toppen

CAPSTONE PRESS
a capstone imprint

Little Pebble is published by Capstone Press,
1710 Roe Crest Drive, North Mankato, Minnesota 56003
www.mycapstone.com

Copyright © 2018 by Capstone Press, a Capstone imprint. All rights reserved. No part of this publication may be reproduced in whole or in part, or stored in a retrieval system, or transmitted in any form or by any means, electronic, mechanical, photocopying, recording, or otherwise, without written permission of the publisher.

Library of Congress Cataloging-in-Publication Data
Names: Wheeler-Toppen, Jodi, author.
Title: Our mouths can taste / by Jodi Wheeler-Toppen.
Description: North Mankato, Minnesota : Capstone, [2018] | Series: Our
   amazing senses | Audience: Age 4-7. | Audience: K to grade 3. | Includes
   bibliographical references and index.
Identifiers: LCCN 2017005233 (print) | LCCN 2017006587 (ebook)
ISBN 9781515767077 (library binding)
ISBN 9781515767169 (paperback)
ISBN 9781515767213 (eBook PDF)
Subjects: LCSH: Taste—Juvenile literature. | Mouth—Juvenile literature. |
   Senses and sensation—Juvenile literature.
Classification: LCC QP456 .W46 2018 (print) | LCC QP456 (ebook) | DDC
   612.8/7—dc23
LC record available at https://lccn.loc.gov/2017005233

Editorial Credits
Abby Colich, editor; Juliette Peters, designer; Wanda Winch, media researcher;
Tori Abraham, production specialist

Photo Credits
Dreamstime: Monkey Business Images, 21; iStockphoto: NathanMarx, 7, svetikd, 19;
Shutterstock: agsandrew, motion design element, Aniko Hobel, 15 (bottom), BW Folsom,
17 (top right), Christian Jung, 17 (top left), GOLFX, 1, hanapon1002, 11, Monkey Business
Images, 13, Nathalie Speliers Ufermann, 9 (inset), Preto Perola, 15 (top), Rabus Carmen Olga,
5, Robyn Mackenzie, 17 (bottom), Yulia Kozlova, cover; Thinkstock: Photodisc/Keith Brofsky, 9

Table of Contents

Take a Bite!

It is time to eat.

You have an apple.

Mmm. How does it taste?

In Your Mouth

You take a bite. Then chew.

Food and spit mix.

Spit helps you taste.

Look at your tongue.

Can you see the bumps?

The bumps have taste buds.

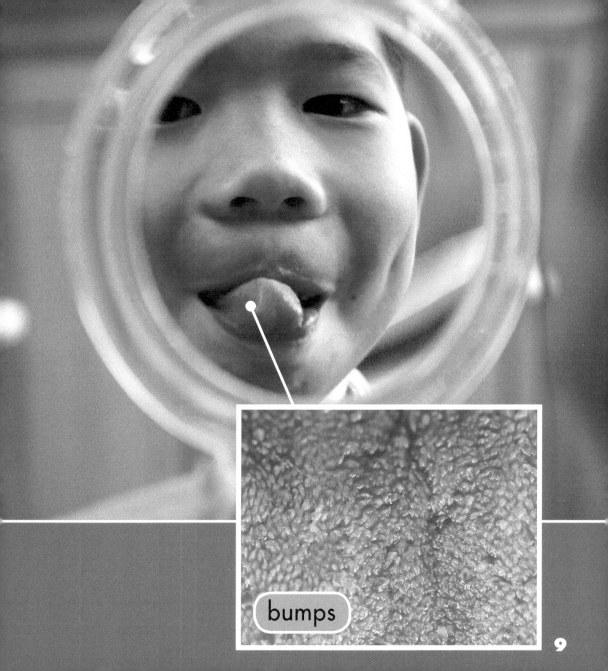

bumps

Now you swallow.

Food goes to the throat.

Taste buds are there too.

Taste buds have cells.

They signal your brain.

It knows the taste.

Yum! Yum!

The apple is sweet.

Fun Food

We can taste five flavors.

Sweet is one.

Salty is one too.

sweet

salty

15

We taste sour.

We taste bitter. **Ick! Ick!**

We taste umami too.

sour

bitter

umami

Some foods have a smell.

Smell helps you.

It lets you taste.

Do you like fish?

Eww! No!

Here is cake. **Oh! Yes!**

Your mouth lets you taste.

Glossary

bitter—very harsh or unpleasant

brain—the organ inside your head that controls your movements, thoughts, and feelings

cell—the smallest unit of a living thing

signal—a message between the brain and the senses

sour—having a sharp, acidlike taste, such as a lemon

taste bud—a small organ in the mouth that tells people what things taste like

umami—a taste found in meat and cheese

Read More

Appleby, Alex. *What I Taste.* My Five Senses. New York: Gareth Stevens Publishing, 2015.

Dayton, Connor. *Taste.* Your Five Senses and Your Sixth Sense. New York: PowerKids Press, 2014.

Rustad, Martha E.H. *Tasting.* Senses in My World. Minneapolis, Minn.: Bullfrog Books, 2015.

Internet Sites

Use FactHound to find Internet sites related to this book.

Visit *www.facthound.com*
Type in this code: 9781515767077

Check out projects, games and lots more at
www.capstonekids.com

Critical Thinking Questions

1. How does spit help you taste?

2. What would happen if your tongue had no taste buds?

3. Reread page 16. Use the glossary to define one of the flavors we can taste.

Index